AF412125

Kathleen Spivack

Swimmer in the Spreading Dawn

Apple-wood Books   Cambridge/Newton   1981

Swimmer in the Spreading Dawn © 1981 Kathleen
Spivack

ISBN: 0-918222-24-9

All rights reserved. Printed in the United States of America.
No part of this book may be used or reproduced in any
manner whatsoever without written permission, except in
the case of brief quotations embodied in critical articles and
reviews. For information write to Apple-wood Books, Box
2870, Cambridge, Massachusetts 02139.

For Nova and Marin

Swimmer in the Spreading Dawn

ACKNOWLEDGMENTS

The author would like to thank the editors of the following in which these poems first appeared:

(bathing the children/ a geology lesson) **Transatlantic Review**; (small letters) **The Atlantic Monthly**; (Hello) **Esquire**; (The System) **Kayak**; (Short Stories) **Ploughshares**; (The evening plane to Bridgeport) **The New Yorker**; (smoke) **Esquire**; (Greenish) **American Poetry Review**; (Our Town) **American Poetry Review**; (Traveling Away) **American Poetry Review**; (Flowers) **Ploughshares**; (Blue Movies) **Agenda**; (the way it is) **13th Moon**; (Tide-wife) **Esquire**; (Photography as Effect of Light) **American Poetry Review**; (Five Women) **Ploughshares**; (The Blouse) **Esquire**; (The Abandoned Baby) **Dark Horse**; (rose moss) **Dark Horse**; (marble) **Poetry Now**; (Raceway) **Poetry Now**; (all night) **American Poetry Review**; (lifting up) **Pourboire**; (Semantics) **Kayak**; (snow and) **Agenda**; (Work) **The Hudson Review**; (Breath) **Green House**; (The glass bottle) **Poetry Now**; (Flight) **The Blacksmith**; (The Alarm) **The Lamp in the Spine**; (The Dreamer) **The Lamp in the Spine**; (Who flees) **Poetry Now**; (january thaw) **The Atlantic Monthly**; (The Fourth of July) **Poetry Now**; (The mountain wife) **Alaluz**; (every morning) **The Blacksmith**; (I want to tell you) **Paris Review**; (The Frost Farm) **The Real Paper**; (Approaching the Canvas) **The Real Paper** reprinted in **Tendril**; (Daphne) **The Partisan Review**; (the dark) **Poetry Now**; (figure/ground) **Small Moon**; (Flowers) **Ploughshares**; (Fugue) **American Poetry Review**; (meditation) **The Massachusetts Review**; (Sleeping next to you in North Dakota) **The Massachusetts Review**; (Wild animals in houses) **American Poetry Review**; (Swimmer in the Spreading Dawn) **Kayak**.

Special appreciation to the National Endowment for the Arts, The Massachusetts Artist's Foundation, and the Howard Foundation for their generous assistance which provided the time to work on these poems.

CONTENTS

IV. Struggling for Air

V. Open Windows

I. Dusk

bathing the children/ a geology lesson

sweet
   bathwater, skimmy
   and green:

body
   detritus laps circles
   round the tub.

my children
   slough off their skins here,
   skittering, joyfully as soap.

watching them,
   the mirror clouds
   with reflective breath

rising as
   their rounded bodies,
   islands, rise

steaming,
   veined with the
   imprint of ferns upon stone.

12

small letters

the leaves change
the trees do not change
I am waiting here
on your front porch, giving up.

inside, the rooms are saying
you have no messages for me:
a shoe on the step
an overturned deck

chair; it is the end
of summer, goodbye.
the doorbell is ringing
your telephone is ringing

I am trying to tell you
there are still some connections
and you stand in your kitchen,
silent, wiping your hands.

figure/ground

standing still
I observe you
as if already writing the script
of my own flight from you.
you are the gentle one
I have been seeking.
abandoned to strangers,
despised

I have lived among danger
for many years
I have grown accustomed
now the sky turns silver
it is a rackham illustration
it is a fairy tale

in which I am innocent
and lovely,   in which the wind
makes many mouths
blowing cold   in which I'm
defenseless
sheltering in a tree

I must wait out the storms
and the evil spirits
I must do many chores
before I am loved
and even the reward is not a sure thing.
my tears fall

14

I learn to carry water
I burn my own body for warmth
I hug only myself and think of parents.
in the night, goblins
climb out of the bare ground
and pull my hair
they say I am ugly
and must starve, chop wood,

and conceal pain.
I draw back
but come to believe the dark
the wildness of survival,
persecution
and the screeching of

large birds.
one day, following
pebbles backward carefully
I come upon you
in the clearing.
the trees signal me
"this is it," they whisper
"this is your chance."
but I have never heard

the sound of a human
voice
nor seen
a person who resembles
me, except in the pond
while washing my clothes
so when you speak

I tremble
like a deaf-mute
hiding from you when at the same
time I am longing,
pressing myself to myself
like a deer or a stone
or a wild creature
with whom you are not familiar.

16

I want to tell you

Sitting and writing on the dining room table,
I want to tell you what it is to be alive:
the yellow oilcloth cover takes the imprint
of my thoughts;   the tablecloth reads back

"I want." The mark of my pen
presses on the floral print: "I want to tell."
An explosion of daisies stands fading
in the flower pot, a used Dundee marmalade

jar, ivory. The ordinary daisies, as steadfast as a
woman, hold their yellow centers: he loves me,
loves me not;   he picks me as he
likes: he steps on me.

The daisies make a still life
next to sour apples and, rotting
in a green bowl, artistic
sour lemons. They are trying

to look yellow. The children
are crying "We want milk" at the door. It
is dark, the sky's uneasy; it will rain.
The swallows' repetitions

swooping through my ears, the note
of the bobwhite, calling in the bushes,
remains, I feel, long after
any sound I make has gone:

when my hands have done the dishes;
after I've recorded what it's like to mop the floor.
Why do I keep so clean, like all the other
animals? Why do I worry

if the children lie too thickly
dreaming their dreams, in a heavy sleep
like fog? I write so much
on the inside of my brain

that I forget what it was
that I wanted to tell you. But
through the open door, warm
white rose petals blow in.

18

Hello

I say, didn't I see you at Tahoe?
My. That was many years ago.
But didn't we have a fine time then?
All gone.   All gone.

Excuse me, didn't we meet at Estes?
My, wasn't it cold that summer?
My wife remembers you from the hotel.
Oh yes.   How do you do.

Don't you remember, at Silver Lake?
The dresses I wore that year, so lovely.
They used to have those canoes we took out.
Oh no.   That was Saratoga Springs.

Say, didn't we dance at Asbury Park?
That was a long time ago.   Twenty nine?
You were the best dancer out on the floor.
I don't remember dancing with you.

Don't you remember at Tahoe, the lake—
Yes, it used to be so clear. So sad.
That's my wife sitting over there.
My legs aren't what they used to be.

Hey, remember on the Queen Mary, that summer?
We shared a stateroom, we shared the same bed.
We spent the night drinking and watching the sea.
So sorry.   I hardly remember you.

The System

First
wipe your feet, before you
come in.

Now clean your plate,
then you can have
a cookie.

Be a good boy, say
your prayers. Now
come give mommy a kiss.

Pick up your
room; then you can go to the
game with Harry.

Just finish
school, then we'll
see. Wait

till you're married, then you
can stick her all you
want.

Prove yourself
first: get a job.
Later,

think about cars, your own
home. Put in your time
during the week:

Saturday night,
go out for a beer
with the boys.

Save up a bundle: vacations
come later. First
get them through college—

(plenty of time
when that's done.) Pay
off the bills and insurance,

then move to our
Home for the
Aging.

We've built it right next to
the Framingham Dump,
so

first dump your
garbage. Then come
visit us.

Short Stories

I am writing my heart out here.
In a kitchen two towns away,
my friend Fanny is doing likewise.

She sits surrounded by her children
like a patient plant.
When we telephone each other

the children come into our ears
like static; stereo commotion:
they cling to us like clay.

When we sit down to write—
three hours each morning—our children
put their damp hands on us

like tendrils; someone is always falling down.
The children come to us,
beasts needing to be gentled.

Fanny speaks to them wispily;
her pale blonde face is tired.
Late afternoons she creeps away to brood.

She writes violent purple stories about
women submitting;   fortissimo despair;
incredible bed scenes: love never works out

for the people of Fanny's mysterious prose.
Then she gets up and changes a diaper;
her toddlers are restless, they want to go out.

She closes the notebook; she raises
her head as from a fuschia daze:
writing such stories is like immersion;

living her daily life is like a dream.
And her characters, frozen, wait between pages
for Fanny to finish, the children in bed,

and come back to them in racked exhaustion
to mark with her pen on inscrutable pages
passion, suffering, extraordinary lives.

The evening plane to Bridgeport

It's as if you'd taken the roof
off everybody's lives:
the tennis players running,
white on green,
the baseball game below, its process
slow and deliberate as chewing gum,
the houses
that would flake if you
fell on them, or thought
so: mothers
calling you homeward,
dusky end of day;
through estuaries, harbors
packed with boats, the bright
green marshes leaving
you behind
and flying, flying
into the setting shine.

24

the caller

you are pursuing me
like a pervert through the telephone
there's no getting away
you will find me out

I send out petalled signals
pouring pine scent in my footsteps
I throw smoke behind me
footsteps grudging as breadcrumbs:

polite footsteps, a woman moving away.
I don't give out my number
I unlist my eyelashes
I blacklist my secrets

and still I don't say anything
significant.   you are calling me up:
"hello again."
the phone sizzles with energy

I hold it away from me
I refuse to feel anything,
you want me to do what you want
me to do. I do everything except hang up.

Greenish

It seems to grow darker.
It seems there is rain coming.
The rustle of trees is insistent: hear me.

I feel you
wanting to move towards me
in the darkening kitchen.

The pigeons and
other birds of Watertown
give off warning salutes

and the town tennis players run
faster, racing the storm. Their ball,
skidding across the net,

glows phosphorus. Your serve.
Everything takes a deep breath
and holds it.

26

smoke

take out the buildings, put in trees,
landscapes, hills: insurrectionist

curves.   take out the
smog, set the clear note

of the tuba, winding round and round;
take out the

figures put in ground.

put in: sky, shrugs of shoulders, silences
(take out hustling)

take out roads, leave leaves.
take out indians.   put in.

let the leaves come on
like a rushing of uncontrolled love;

faraway   faraway

let a bird, let a silver
river, spill.

II. Night Gardenias

Our Town

Listen, at night you can hear the leaves
falling open like babies' hands:
all along the branches, secret buds.

Around here the flowers
explode open, star like,
with nearly inaudible pops.

Stand still. You can hear earthworms
chewing their way through clotted leaves:
the leaf pile shrugs, unsettled.

Down the hill, trucks
shift gears to other destinations
but our neighborhood is seething with life.

Our two streets embrace under the street light;
the earth tilts a little more leftward;
under the blue quilt, our bodies jigsaw and fit.

30

Traveling Away

Feelings muffle.
I get on the ferry:
the boat pulls out
from here to there.

On an aerial map
the islands stand out
like patches of fur.
The north wind is so earnest.

Suppose I were cut off
from you forever,
floating on this ocean
flatly, everything in abeyance.

The water spins off
like the inside of a marble;
seagulls shriek **forget:**
being alone again is like dreaming.

My hands and feet throb warmly;
heavy wind tries to beat me down.
Cold on the foredeck I wonder
what it'd be like with the skipper

who grinds a cigar
as he works at the wheel;
what it's like drifting
from home to away,

sleeping from island to island
until this green harbor enters
me. Now the boat tenses;
they get out the lines,

waking into the great
pilings, shuddering and easing.
I startle towards you.
I begin to look for a telephone.

32

Flowers

Regarding the insides of flowers:
this is something about which I have meant
to write you for a long time.

How awkwardly, but to a bee
fascinating it must seem, going in
to their sticky centers, half-

repellent, touching
their furry genitalia;   horrible
to love and seek so, being dependent: .

flowers' perfectly formed
hemispheres, the pretend in-
sistence on privacy

like the hidden ladyslipper, modest,
shocking, sudden labia
blushing,

bifurcated, veined and
obvious: it is so soft,
slipping in,

is it not, and out?
I too am always
obsessed with the insides of flowers,

yearning to plunge
a finger into them
or a metaphor:

the "hermaphroditic artist"
invading the subject;
shivering at anemones,

at their dark secret
centers, or the double wheel
within a poppy, spoked

mouth slit and laughing.
The "Language of Flowers,"
spoken, translates "Sex."

If a daylily bends in the vase
it means: she is waiting.
If straight: trouble ahead.

If the flowers persist
in their drooping
throw them out

but refurbish
for it is good to have fresh
flowers beside one, breathing

their bodily secrets
by night, cleverly accessible
and bedded, moist.

34

the way it is

He is called "clinically depressed":
he can't make a living.

She is: supportive; un-
derstanding; kind.   A shrew,

an anxious nag.   A
mom.   She

loves him, wants
to leave.   Check

one. Check all.
They wait for

news.   They don't
buy meat.   Still milk

is on the table, powdered,
dried.   She goes to work;

the children stand in the door,
staring at him.

All day he sits,
head in his hands,

no work.   He asks,
What's wrong with

me?   The shrink
says: fifty dollars

please.   His daughters
need their teeth

fixed.   So it's
no more shrink, no

teeth.   The rent
goes up,

the lights go down,
the heat goes

down: their hearts
turn off.   In bed

he makes no moves,
nor she, listening to his

breathing, in
and out, till morning.

36

Blue Movies

We're sitting here, watching a movie
in which an actress goes down on the hero, hard.
There is no sound from the huddle
of the theatre, the lights
are dim, and outside, it's rain-
ing. Sitting here is like being underground,

and on the set, too, it's raining. Ground
out, these flickering porno movies
are as predictable, as wet as rain.
I try not to watch, but it's hard
not to sense it: the sex, the light
limbs entangling, that huddle

of hair and hands. Huddling
next to each other, we avoid common ground,
keep watching the dirty movie
as a way of flinching from lights.
Outside, it is steadily rain-
ing: not getting excited is hard;

loving you, even harder.
Later, at home, we will huddle
together, watching the images rain
on our eyes and replay them, ground
out ironically, once the lights
are switched on. Our own life's a movie

played backwards: the reels move
more slowly, reversed. Scene One: he gets hard;
he goes limp. Scene Two: she falls light-
ly asleep. Waking later, huddled
in darkness beside him, she hears the ground
note, held and repeated, persistent as rain,

and stays awake, listening. It's still raining.
The film ends now. Walking out of the movie,
sleepwalkers, nervous, we cover old ground,
clutching our umbrellas, huddling,
and by necessity together. Staying married is hard
when, beyond us, shimmering, light

bodies leap and beckon. We huddle, blinking. Too much light!
In the dark it's less hard, living close to the ground,
making home movies, and seeping into each other like rain.

38

Tide-wife

This small house
protects you from the sea;
you stay in the kitchen, waiting.

Outside, the buildings
huddle along the harbor.
Your hands stiffen;

miser, you cannot open them.
Near the deserted candy booth
the ferry comes in, once

a day, hooting,
widening its fruitful maw:
footsteps exclaim in this little town.

You close yourself off from the wind
that is like anger, tugging
at your arms. You close

all the doors
and tell me: "I
am ordering seeds;

I am learning
to sew. I have friendship
here, not the unrest of

passion." Pressing
your knuckles to your mouth
you tame yourself

and the wind
washes through Provincetown
like bitter herbs,

like water
roaring up over the jetty,
and the sky changes, winter,

and women like you wait
in squat white houses
for warmth to enter them,

for the sea to take over
and say it all, sending in
bouquets of white froth,

for words, sinking
like leaky lifeboats,
for the moon, howling, refusing

to be held in; for someone,
drowning out at sea,
sending you his death.

40

the other

she rides up at night
when only the horses hear her
they stir, uneasy in the stable
a cloud covers the moon

she enters the bedroom
she enters your sleeping brain
as you lie beside me
your hand touching my hip

and she whispers
"rise up."   you leave your body
you leave yourself sleeping beside me
you leave those ears of corn, our children

your hand trembles and then stops
but otherwise you do not stir
as I move slightly nearer
your shadowed right side

the dark horses whinny warnings
but only the reluctant animals wake up
she touches your dream places, stranger,
everything else goes back to sleep again

in the darkness together
you do a strange dance, absenting;
next to me you are here and not here
like a riddle: it gets harder seeming real

A Short

You groan and sob above me like a woman;
your black eyes have forgotten
who it is you are screwing.

Now we're both carved up on a diagram:
"erogenous zones."
But the lights go dead.

I can't read my own text.
You are shaking the bed with an insistent
vigor. "Listen to me," you are saying

from someplace faraway.
The pages of the sheets tonight
warn me to close this book.

Photography as the Effect of Light

Your body, a stooped critical question mark:
what is the meaning? You are looking
through thick plate glass
at me, at the children,
hoping the lens
will make us larger than we are,

so faraway and bright.
More focused than we should be, we recede.
The children wave.
You see their moonlit faces;
blinking, you make them disappear
onto the screen:
you are trying so hard to love!

Now you're the projectionist as well.
I'm standing in a field of daisies,
skirt blowing, shading my eyes
from your penetrating glare.
I hold our children's hands:
the movie slows
and in a burst of flower-like flecks
the film goes dark. Your view of us,
your brain, the flashbulb, blows.

Sleeping next to you in North Dakota

Tunneling into the prairie
you hide yourself still further,
white on white.
All around you it moves
in its awful whiteness:
the deliberate trees are planted
and marshall in rows,
not concealing. Few bare houses,
the snow aches,
the black dirt disagrees.
At the edges of the dish
grain elevators jut out
under this helpless span, the sky;
potato fields;
and you are even more helpless:
you whimper like a child
or a dog.

No one in the silence hears you:
the terrible fields
stretch out, lying down
like your vulnerable body;
you want to be loved
but nothing comes close
in this outreach, marching
right-angled.
This is a dream without touch
in which you are screaming
throughout sleep.
Your lips part, silent,
and your twitching body
settles further, stilled.

44

The roads are four-cornered,
mute and interchangeable:
there are no centers
in this country of cold
where even my distances
don't reach you.

III. Staying Up Alone

Wild animals in houses

In the evenings
the animals come into the houses
and fold themselves,
furred, on the beds.   The deer
sheds bitter tears,
looking at vacant
distance.   Bears
on their separate
ice floes, pacing,
sigh through their sleep.   They dream
of a setting in which
they are no longer artifice.
Down the hall the
toilets flush.   A cough .
Then all is silent, covert again.
A spider monkey
bites her paw: **don't
come too close.**
Slight lemurs wake
to wonder where and
why they are, briefly,
studying night vision.
Sleep drifts up like snow.
The lion moans
but no one touches.   Nurse-
attendants turn off the hall light.
Rooms, so self contained, expand
and float away whitely.
Now the cool odor of the rose

48

garden presses the windows
softly, entering like dawn.
O longings of wild
animals stirring,
lifting the flying
far off houses,
stealing the night!

Five Women

Five women, talking while spring
came: petals of the hand;
the whispering of rain.

One talked of loneliness;   sudden
alarm: four startled
deer leapt into

the distance.   One measured
the spirit the length of the
night, a seismograph charting

the rising of tremors.   One
of her husband thought always/   his
absence, her heart

sheathed in grief, a hy-
acinth.   And one, with trembling
hands, said nothing,

chaste and severe
as an easter lily.
The fifth

ran home in haste to her
lover, hot as the sun
in her ardent bed.

50

The Blouse

I telephoned a friend:
she was living with a man from
Sweetheart Plastics:

quick, hang up the phone,
I am burning for you!
She unbuttons for him

while she talks with me:
her body has a mind
of its own. It performs

exquisitely, though her ear
has married the phone
and is the still point

for her moist gyrations.
What has both
tensile strength

and flex? Sweetheart,
he pleads,
hang up the

phone. Put those
bendable arms
'round my columnar neck

and let's make it. Make it!
Just a minute, she says,
sucking a pencil:

she widens her eyes;
molding herself to the phone,
and hardens.

52

winter storm by the ocean

mist on white horses
mist on the water

the white snow-mist blowing
mist on the dune grass

snow on the cattails
the brown reeds bending

mist on our faces
the white swans escalating

mist on a flight of ducks
honking out over water crests

like quarrels our last nignt
I am forgetting why

mist on the outlines, a huddle
of hills, the shore

faraway fading like memory
blown through the mind

while the thick ponies stand
in a shaggy field; white silences

The Abandoned Baby

All day in the crib the sunlit bars
slatted from left wall to right wall;
the angles grew sharper but no one came:
I played with the shadows of my fingers.

All night in the darkness, suffocating,
I breathed my sour terror in and out;
by morning I slept again, listless:
whichever prism day came next I lay through.

No footstep on the stair, no hurry, no comfort;
no larger body in sun-smelling clothes
to honey me to her softness: nothing moved
but my heartbeat, its cavernous persistence

training itself not to want.
Watchful, I stared at the corners
of things; the whole room flowering awake—
I am fading into my own absence.

54

Semantics

I want to write
from the children's hospital
but it is hard
from this position.
They have tied me to

a bed, spread-
eagled, needles in my
arms. I scream
but no one ever comes.
At night

the babies cry
mommy, mommy, like star-
fish;   a pulse in the corridors:
lights and soft
shoes.

They untie me
to eat: I tend to
the cool chink of ice
in my mouth. They bathe
me: that is the nicest part,

sitting up.
Then I fall back into
darkness.   I have discovered
my own mind and that
is terrible:

I have discovered
what it means to be Conscious,
lying here alone,
nobody's warm arms
and mother gone.

It is being forgotten.
When they let her in, days,
I press my hot pain
to her breast
and pretend to be little again.

Closing time, when she
leaves,   pinioned,
I lie in the web; tied,
hands and feet to the
crib's iron sides,

sobbing and
calling.   Out of this dark
void called Fever, called
Giving Up, they teach me
this is what is meant by Getting Better.

56

rose moss

rose moss/   her real
name.

her blown soul an eager
rose in rain.

rose moss: her soul a sealed
hermetic emblem.

spring rose
moss/ · the pave-

ment's fragrant, small
struck leaves

earth-smell.
distressed, she says

I have no where
to turn

she says, blushing,
I will change my life;

she glitters
with an obsession

for growing.
each tiny fern-like sprig

of sensibility
makes her green whole

and she waits, closed, she
waits, breathing upward.

58

snow and

snow and
I must spend more time alone.

up the street
the husbands are going freelance,

hunched into
third floor rooms, hairy

and writing, writing.
there is the clatter of branches: trees

freeze.   there is
no other way to support this life

than by going
solitary;   obsessing the great

american novel—or scrawling
pornies in new england while the snow

settles.   others go out to work.
closing down on their jobs, the streets

fill up,
ice themselves in.   there is no

getting away;
there is only suffocation:

as in these
words spilling themselves into attics;

this
wife and these children, hungrily

quiet, patiently
waiting, housebound downstairs.

60

Work

She squeezes backseat in their car; her camera lies
clamped between her legs. They speed into the country.
She is the prisoner of two fortyish married lovers
who have hired her to watch and photograph
and celebrate their loving, writing
on negatives forever their deliberate coupling.

Swaddled, she hugs herself, observing the couple:
the man drives, the wife says nothing. The road lies
straight through the woods. He knows the right
road by heart; exactly how to penetrate this country.
Now he stops the car. The nervous woman photographer
imagines how they will be, making love.

Unlocking the house, they enter, giggling.   Love,
the trio knows, is what they're here for. Of the couple,
he appears more eager. He undresses. Photographs
of him come easily. They position themselves, lie
down together. She pulls shades. In the stillness of the country,
the photographer turns lights on, for the rite

demands bare angles, naked light. Now she checks the right
exposure, reading sex on her emulsions: the lovers
moan at her, strangers, from another country.
And she clicks, fixed to her lens, registering the couple
but trying not to hear them. Her gaze lies
flat against her camera.   She photographs

their heat as composition. Sex is a photograph
of strangers, sinuous. Terrified, she writes
it down on film. She's spellbound while they lie
beneath her, working rapidly. They writhe, make love
more loudly now, on camera. Shooting the couple,
she starts to shake, standing in their country

house, trying not to enter, concentrating, their country
of mutual stimulation. Later, developing the photographs,
she observes the rinsed emerging couple
entangled systematically in sequence. Love
has never looked so cold, a teeth-bared animal rite
in focus, without meaning. But the photographs don't lie.

They lie in her darkroom, drying, always right.
In a country of couples, only she is truly in love,
they tell her, alone with her fixatives, her photographs.

62

The Frost Farm in Derry, New Hampshire

Robert Frost, your homestead in Derry, New
Hampshire is a mess:
the orchard out back has been cut down;
the ground has been stripped of its topsoil

and is an auto wrecking yard.
In the moonlight the subsoil glitters like Christmas
with cracked windshields; discarded tires
wreathe the mounds where apple trees once stood.

Route 28 passes right out in front.
I lay awake, acquainted all one night
with the upstairs front bedroom
where you listened to the breathing of your children

in nineteen oh seven.
Now diesel trucks and souped-up cars shift gears
by the front door. They are more deafening than rain.
There is a trailer camp across the way

where you used to do all that meeting and passing.
The brook's a brown polluted stink.
It's impossible to get hired help;
and they've torn out your kitchen to make it

workable. They have moved in a fellow
who says he is a poet.
But who knows? This poet has a wife
who isn't in the least a silken tent

nor he. Living on food stamps, they are
substantial human beings
who don't know a damn thing
about farming.

A tramp came to the door today,
some bearded hippie from out west named Patrick,
who thinks you're the greatest.
This fellow hitchhiked all the way from Montana

to see this place where you lived and worked.
Now Patrick, the poet and the wife
are sitting in the green remodeled kitchen
in what used to be your farmhouse

and rapping (that's the word
they use these days) about you,
Robert Frost, you lousy farmer,
who sold this farm and got out of New Hampshire

the minute your grandfather's will said you could.
This farm's so mean and poor no one could make it pay
so you did what you could do best which was to write,
(and some of the walls you mended are still standing.)

When you finally sold the Derry farm you wrote:
"It shall be no trespassing/ If I come again some spring
In the gray disguise of years/Seeking ache of memory here."
The new owner auctioned the topsoil to make the downpayment;

later he sold to the auto wrecking yard. That's progress,
I guess. But you were so paradoxical
you were to look back on that hen scratching
in Derry as in an idyll

in a long line of insanities and death.
("What but design of darkness to appall?")
The first child died and was buried in the snow
but four slept still in a safe white whisper.

I should be telling you this in perfect metrics:
an approximation of the heart will have to do.
To suffer so much and still to go on writing
was either famous Frost perversity or courage.

Years later, after your wife had died,
she sent you back with her ashes to scatter them.
You drove up to the door on the highway home
and found the farm scarred by strangers, irretrievably.

And you turned away with the ashes past the house,
past the broken glass, the wreckage, the ruined fields,
and walked out on New Hampshire for the second time,
to sleep in America forever.

IV. Struggling for Air

Breath

Struggling for air—
in Woods Hole it is four o'clock
in the morning.
I am with you
not because I want to be,
the grey air chilling the strange room,
but because I am.

No questions: the heaped clothes
are as bewildered
as my own night tangle.
It seems I can't breathe
though outside this dark
house, the ocean
breathes by itself;
relentless, flat, and dominant.

What am I doing here,
married?
I am smothering
on my own asthmatic
childhood; a foghorn wheezes:
estrangement
near the underwater rocks.

68

Approaching the Canvas

She is getting too big. They live in two rooms.
Mother sends her to the Y to learn to paint.
She crayons, she draws pictures labelled "Mother."
She draws the narrow view from her open
window: the sooty roofs of Brooklyn, the sky
smudged.   She has trouble focusing

but she tries to keep her life in focus:
the small apartment, the vast dotted rooms
of the museums where each vision of sky
becomes a postage stamp of nature. The paintings
tell her to dare more, to open
her eyes.   But she holds on to her mother.

At night in her dreams she calls "Mother"
and her mouth does not move. Only her brain is in focus.
She dreams she is downstairs, opening
a door. She walks into a cellar, through the boiler room
and shoulders her way through a corridor. No sky
here, no light by which to paint

what her blind fingers feel. Cracked paint
pulls her through a narrow hallway. Her mother
recedes into background: the perspective is on sky
pulling her forward; triangular, edging into focus
her blurred dreams. The close room
suffocates. She suffers like birth, hunching toward open

sunlight. The tunnel ends, pushing open
into a technicolor vista like landscape painting
singing, tenderness.   Here there is room
for her pomegranate being. Her mother,
black and white, is calling from the background. She focuses
precisely on the present: the cerulean sky,

the sun like petals, the sky
jubilant as her body, opening.
Green fields spread out, like walking into a painting
of her own mind; all her childhood focuses
on this moment, the narrow room
giving way to larger doorways. Even her mother

fades. Flowering, focused, now this girl cries "Mother,"
frightened. She opens herself: there is too much room
in the sky. And she paints a small corner.

70

The glass bottle

I breathe messages into your body
as into a glass bottle.
You sleep on: an entire model ship
flowers inside you,
full sail, impenetrable. There is no way
of reaching you;
I am caught in the shoals
by your dappled beaches.

A castaway, sending obscure and
flailing calls for help,
I seal my silent
nightmares, stopper them,
transparent next to you.

If you happen to find
Kathleen Spivack
adrift, please
give her my love
and return to
53 Spruce Street
Watertown, Massachusetts
oh two one seven two.

marble

when you sat up on the side of the bed
it was as if you had killed me.
(the hyperbole here of seeing myself bleeding.)
I lay in my circle, meek and solitary,
you ebbing away from me letting you do it.

I could be sleeping forever, you inside me,
an unbroken tantric daydream:
never to wake and walk away—
what mush! what garbage to write
over a man—you were simply getting up.
you are withdrawing further and further.

Raceway

The driveway recedes behind you;
I stand here with the children, getting smaller.
The old car kicks up dust;
you're obscuring us:
naked, we avert our faces.

Your face is pressing itself forward, resolute:
you jut out onto the home stretch like a maniac.
The wheels spin, you will yourself to
stop loving,
accelerator pressed to the floor,

refusing to turn back.
From here on, your oases are plastic
restaurants, rest rooms, and ice cream cones:
ninety miles an hour
beats the speed limit for forgetting.

The noise of the motor
drowns out all goodbyes
behind you: with a wrench
the brakes give way
and you careen

suddenly faster, in tightening
circles. A panic! Your feet press
"stop" and also "start." You are crossing
the line, a runaway winner.

Flight

In the airport,
rows of fixed chairs, primly.
I have left our children behind.

The warmth of your touch
is no longer immediate:
my body

has its own second nature.
I rearrange it
into right angles, sitting

alone for once, my arms
at my sides and waiting.
This silence

is good for getting
ideas in: its folds
an arrangement

of schedules and destinations. But
my ideas seem less important;
you, the children,

74

fly backwards
away from me—
or is it, me from you,

all of us,
skyward, looking on
and getting smaller?

The Alarm

The sudden bray of a firehorn
(like a shock of recognition.)
At the fire house, firemen
struggle into their clothes.

They put out cigarettes:
the sirens, green, insist.
The flop of heavy slickers;
"uh" as they strain into their boots.

Across town, ladies,
skinny-armed like furniture,
fling tables and chairs
through the open shouts of windows
crying "Don't let mother's linen burn!"

This way! This way!
The rooftops sizzle.
Men, red and silver, move
on great machines. The midnight streets
chug only in one direction.
The air is round with a terrible vacancy—
I am embracing the wrong person.

76

The Dreamer

You are the one who, sleeping, climbs out onto rooftops:
the one who, refusing the coffin,
moves from narrow side to bony side
and then lifts up. The top of the house
flips open like a dollhouse;   lets you
enter the sky.

You clamber up the chimney
and in this dream your legs are bare
and hairy. The moon makes little glow
and your beard waggles. You stretch:
you are living out your dreams

"unhealthily," as the psychiatrists would say.
You start to crow, then pantomime elaborate
shushing, tiptoe on the rooftops
of the city. You are the one with vision.
Jumping from building to building,
you open each hinged roof,

shimmying down between the rafters.
You enter the women.
They sleep through you, forever in white night-
gowns. Their lips part,
and otherwise they do not signify
you, but for their quickened breathing.

Who flees

Now there is no trust between us.
I haven't lain down in a green
clearing.
I haven't given you
a single thought to hurt
me with:
I am deciding whether to leave.

Only there is no place to leave **to**:
parting the tall grasses, signals,
running through a field.
Always in my mind I am
running towards you
even when I am most
running away.

The grasses quiver in the sharp
sun; the daisies
and indian paintbrush
stiffen again, bright stabs,
and this painting closes over,
finishing itself.

78

Fugue

Entering the darkened room
where you are playing your flute
imperfectly, the children playing
while a fugue spills from the record
player, I repeat the cadences of hurting:
the phrase, predictable,
is mounting, more intense,
successive times.

Beyond the rectangle of window,
the sea flashes toward me, framed and blue:
it is such perfect happiness, suggested,
I shall never reach.
The notes of the music slip by, silvery
and gasping: your wrong notes
and my uncertainties.

This would make a perfect ending,
I think, breathless: children murmuring,
oblivious, the music
sonorous, baroque, repetitive.
You drive your flute, stumbling, by
ear, or by will,
unable to sight-read the phrasing
and I stare outward at the ocean
making no wrong moves;
no right ones either.

yes

your large hose
is peeing under my window.
the garden looks up gratefully.

inside I am trying to write—
you will never let me alone.

not even if I hurt you
not even if I love you--
I want to leave but I cannot;
I need you the way the lawn

does:
something shameful
in this secret dependence.

80

january thaw

all of a sudden it stays light for longer;
the light is airy, blue; it softens things.
although the tree twigs catch the sun's slant sternly
there is a faint giving in to their ramrod blackness.

it is clear; we fill up like rivers again:
I come to you for your slightest gesture, love.
late afternoons now it stays light for longer:
snow runs in the sides of streets, extravagant hopes.

one forsythia bush outspreading, splurging,
lifts its blossoms up against the snow
like letters drowned by implacable water
or like me, raising my arms to you too soon.

V. Open Windows

82

you are conspiring

you are conspiring to wake me up
you are signing petitions to wake me up
you are collecting signatures

you hire a sound truck
you broadcast in the streets
you knock on every door but mine

you drill into tree trunks
you bug the chandeliers
you put wires in my fruit cocktail

you are conspiring to wake me up
you take notes
you hide your pad under the napkin

you bleed into your pocket
scribbling onto your best suit
everything I say is held against me

the alarm clock presents its evidence
its hands are stopped at once
that flock of sea gulls tattles

daybreak is bugged
you sign away my pillow
my dreams are registered

my dreaming is forbidden
my breathing
is forbidden.   violets

are censored.   dreams
are put in jail, no trial
the state

requires minds willing, purified.
obedient, the roses
shed their petals, put on thorns

the women put on uniform
the sky, after sunrise, wipes away its smile
the streets click their heels

right-angled, military
the buses stop at every corner
and the birds walk, not fly

even private sleep is interrupted
citizen, you cry, **it is imperative**
and you enter my body without knocking.

84

wordless

we rise up,
our bodies have joined;
we don't speak of it.

all night
in the envelope
gluing, un-

gluing; mixing the letters
till the print
of me-on-you, and you-

on-me is smeared;
we fuse,
we say terrible things

to the carbon paper:
talk-talk
like a typewriter keyboard

tapping the bar
till that jumble
of letters and spaces,

looked at,
loses its metal sense
like language:

all night, inarticulate
thoughts without their names,
we lie, jammed.

we don't speak of it.
we begin again:
white paper.

86

A tree etc.

A tree,
an explosion,
a cauliflower.

I dream of you
lying on your back somewhere
dreaming.

You are not
paralyzed.
We flower together.

The tree sends out signals
as I float upward:
hurry,

you are nearly forty.
Its branches
embrace the sky

so passionately little birds
fly out.
And this painting

starts singing like
white curtains in
low-ceilinged rooms:

the windows, when we met.

**The Fourth of July
which is meant to celebrate independence.**

We are completely meaningless, short-lived,
and bright.
All dazzle, our life sifts away.
You touch me, we explode,
and the fireworks drift down
with a burning sadness.

You extinguish me in so many ways
and still I flower
willingly as poppies.
I rise from the ashes,
slit open, sudden morning rose—
awakening: out of this resistant
darkness, shocked, as by my own blood.

88

The mountain wife

You watch the dawn come up
alone;   you worry about having
more children. **Oh mountain,
vessel of my soul.**

The mountain floats, a chunk of
granite: layers of air peel off.   Below,
colors appear;   in the valley
is still a soft fog.

All night he has surrounded you:
in the morning, the sweetness
of exhaustion calling. Light
strikes the glacier. No more.

You are worn out with childgiving,
crouching always before this edifice.
What do the mountains care?
They purify themselves endlessly.

The sun, rising, extends itself
even to you at your kitchen table.
A conception has "taken place";
ordinary day sounds begin.

The Insult Sonnet

"We have a short life span," you shrug, "why fight?"
Listen, you bastard, that ain't no excuse.
I'll match you tooth for tooth till you understand
me, understand? Take back, give in, unsay,
let go or face me, snarling on all fours,
my fierce fur flying. keep your distance please.
I'd rather fight than kiss a guy so rude:
tonight this bed's not big enough for two
so let's go at it. Test me, push for shove,
till I heave you to the floor. You can sleep
on the rug your mother gave you. I will snore
above, in bed, on ironed sheets, and dream
of having you many ways. (Oh, **many** ways.)
And wake to the sound of my own voice crying "More!"

90

all night

all night the wind buffeted the window
I lay in bed
and side-stroked away from you
further out to sea
the storm whimpered, the house shook
I decided I liked my body, swimming,

but not necessarily you, liking it
beside me, critical and anxious.
you tore at my side with your teeth
and when you kissed me
I drew back: it was water
eroding the beach;
it was seacliff anger.

all night the wind whined
like a boatyard repair crew;
it took the curves, the sky,
unbuilding, plank by plank.
I woke to our bodies accidentally
touching   your blank
back floated toward me:
I clung to the wreckage.

every morning

every morning it's like this:
the thrum of the big boats,
the blackbirds chirring "make way, make
way."   every morning
the sun like a silver disc
beats the ocean flat.

every morning the cargo
dreams into port;
the bass of the great boats
pushes the fog aside.
even now the light is changing
to sunlight clanging on the near shore.

coming in on a moment of flotation,
on stand-still, sweet
roses, which never open further:
even now, the children are crying "uh uh"
from their beds.   I ride in gently;
I lay up alongside.

92

Daphne

The only words I know how to write are leaves;
the only way I know how to be is loyal:
one of those women facing the sea and grieving—
it is surprising how much I can keep to myself.

The only dance now is you and me swaying,
trapped like the ancients, caught in the classic frieze:
and now I am running away while you follow,
one hand outstretched, your mouth an O of astonishment.

At the end of the grove the sea sparkles;
the day opens once more as if nothing has happened.
Naked, you pursue me round a ceramic curve
of red and black figures, like the shores of north america.

Who would have thought the old themes could travel so far?
Yet even now in this new land you are betraying me
just as I wait for a god to enter me,
mute, polymorphous; any shape is possible:

just as a relationship of pursuit
is only possible while both of us are moving.
The sea purifies, so why aren't I happy
standing still, hearing a crow call, blotting out my life?

roses

cut
roses, exultant as a
heartbeat;

dark red, almost
black/   blood—
congratulations.

fists,
they open
to an open hand

petalling, waves,
from the pulsing
center.   powie:

roses in the eye!
signalling:
these are for you;

this deep
organismic
outflinging!

94

meditation

holding you
while you tell me you're "suffused" with
royal blue and
flashes of dark red:

it sounds lovely,
my power
to give you color.

I say:
what does it mean?
is this usual
with you:
are you a student of phenomena?

I am a skeptic even while
I love
you;   possibly because.
next to my body, entering and basking,
is a watcher, observing the extremes.

we turn in sunlight, a prism:
you shoot color in all directions
I reflect both inward and outward,
wanting to laugh
and yes
to squeeze you more:
blue absurdity
yellow happiness.

lifting up

green
arms   orange leaves—

morning peels open
like sections of citrus.

a lemon
sun slants   windows wake

and women in nightgowns, waving
rush out on their front steps

crying "avanti" to the postman.
my small

son, lily-of-the-valley, laugh-
ing, raises his fragrant arms to me.

Swimmer in the Spreading Dawn

Sleepers tossing in a moonlit room,
where is it you are rowing to?
Swimmer in the spreading dawn,
what is your question? Where is this pond?

I hold out my hands. They are radiant
as water. You are parting the sheets
and yet nothing moves. We are edging away
from our bodies in the ocean

like phosphorescent particles.
Each small closed face
with its stubborn moth-like yearnings
faintly flutters. We're all leaving

our rooms. We are beating
at the windows.
Some are trying to get back in.
Would it be death, so

to reach light, sizzling?
A sea voyage, in which the earth
is luminous, not round?
What is it we are seeking, swimmers,

sleepers, held in houses?
I am standing in the dark
near the darker edge of water,
entering, entering, as the sky starts to fill.